VISITOR GUIDES TO HAWAI'I

HAWAI'I THIS & THAT

FACTS AND ANSWERS TO MOST FREQUENTLY ASKED QUESTIONS ABOUT THE ISLANDS

LaRue W. Piercy

MUTUAL PUBLISHING

Other Books By The Author:

Hawai'i's Missionary Saga (Mutual Publishing)

Big Island History Makers (previous title—
Hawai'i Island Leaders) (Mutual Publishing)

Hawai'i: Truth Stranger Than Fiction—True Tales of Missionary Troubles and Triumphs Fictionalized in Michener's Hawaii (Mutual Publishing)

Library of Congress Catalog Card Number: 2003109324

This book is an update and amalgamation of *Hawai'i This and That* and *Hawai'i—A Quick Look at Its History*. Revised 1985, 1994, 1998 and 2003.

Design by Mardee Domingo Melton
Eighth Printing, June 2015

ISBN-10: 1-56647-633-X
ISBN-13: 978-1-56647-633-1

Mutual Publishing, LLC
1215 Center Street, Suite 210 • Honolulu, Hawai'i 96816
Ph: (808) 732-1709 • Fax: (808) 734-4094
www.mutualpublishing.com • e-mail: info@mutualpublishing.com
Printed in Korea

Aloha!

ALOHA
is the spiritual key.

ALOHA is the familiar
Hawaiian greeting and farewell.

ALOHA signifies the sentiments of
affection, sympathy, kindness and love.

ALOHA is the native spirit of friendliness and
hospitality — the essence of the Hawaiian culture.

ALOHA represents the Hawaiians' love of life — their art
of living. For their wealth was not in aggressive accumula-
tion of things but in their joy in sharing and giving.

ALOHA to all of you who enjoy and appreciate
Hawai'i — its beauty, its people and its spirit.

LaRue W. Piercy
Kailua-Kona, Hawai'i

Contents

The Hawaiian Islands

Name — Hawaiki or Hawai'i — traditional home (hawa) of Polynesians with iki or i'i (small). Named Sandwich Islands by Capt. James Cook, first European visitor, 1778, for Earl of Sandwich, First Lord of Admiralty (originator of the sandwich) — name obsolete after 1844

Nickname — Aloha State

Flag — Combination of British and American design — British union jack — 8 red, white, blue stripes for 8 main islands — designed for Kamehameha before 1816 — used for kingdom, republic, territory, state

Seal — heraldic shield between Kamehameha and Goddess of Liberty

Motto — Ua mau ke ea o ka 'āina i ka pono: The life of the land is perpetuated in righteousness.

Bird — Nēnē (Hawaiian goose)

Fish — Humuhumunukunukuāpua'a (triggerfish)

Tree — Kukui (candlenut)

Flower — Hibiscus (pua aloalo)

Song — "Hawai'i Pono'ī," composed by King Kalākaua, music by Capt. Henry Berger, royal Hawaiian bandmaster — national anthem 1876 — state anthem 1967

❃ Unique Hawai'i ❃

ONLY STATE WITH

- Land entirely of islands
- A royal palace
- Single, unified school system
- Increasing land area (from volcanic eruptions)
- Commercial coffee crop — Kona, Hawai'i
- Silversword plants — Haleakalā, Mauna Kea, Mauna Loa
- Majority of people non-white — Asians, Polynesians, Filipinos, or mixed.

❃ Some Superlatives ❃

- Longest chain of islands in the world
- Most southerly point in the U.S. — South Point (Ka Lae), Hawai'i
- Largest inactive volcano in the world — Haleakalā, Maui
- Largest active volcano in the world — Kīlauea, Hawai'i
- Largest military command
- Wettest spot on earth — Mount Wai'ale'ale, Kaua'i
- Tallest coconut tree in the U.S. — 92 ft., 5 in., Hilo, Hawai'i

❃ Island Identifications ❃

Island	Color	Flower	Nickname
KAUA'I	Purple	Mokihana (small native, citrus fruit)	Garden Isle Menehune Land
NI'IHAU	White	Pūpū (small shell)	Forbidden Island
O'AHU	Yellow	Ilima	Gathering Place
MOLOKA'I	Green	Kukui (candlenut)	Friendly Isle
MAUI	Pink	Loke lani (small rose)	Valley Isle
LĀNA'I	Yellow	Kauna'oa (native dodder)	Pineapple Island
KAHO'OLAWE	Gray	Hinahina (native heliotrope)	
HAWAI'I	Red	Lehua ('ōhi'a blossom)	Big Island, Orchid Isle

❃ Hawaiian Islands ❃
Distances — Sizes

Island	Distance (miles)	From	Area (sq. miles)	Length (miles)	Width (miles)
KAUA'I	95	O'ahu	553	33	25
NI'IHAU	17-1/2	Kaua'i	73	18	6
O'AHU			608	44	30
MOLOKA'I	22	O'ahu	261	38	10
MAUI	70	O'ahu	729	48	26
LĀNA'I	28	Moloka'i	140	18	13
KAHO'OLAWE	6	Maui	45	11	6
HAWAI'I			4,038	93	76
Kona	170	Honolulu			
	62	Hilo			
Hilo	216	Honolulu			

❋ Hawai'i's People ❋

ETHNIC POPULATION, 2000		
Caucasian	24.3%	294,102
Japanese	16.7%	201,764
Filipino	14.1%	170,635
Native Hawaiian	6.6%	80,137
Chinese	4.7%	56,600
Korean	1.9%	23,537
Black or African American	1.8%	22,003
Vietnamese	0.6%	7,867
Asian Indian	0.1%	1,441
Other Asian	3.5%	42,024
Pacific Islanders	2.7%	33,402
Other Races	1.6%	18,682
Mixed (Two or more races)	21.4%	259,343
Total		**1,211,537**

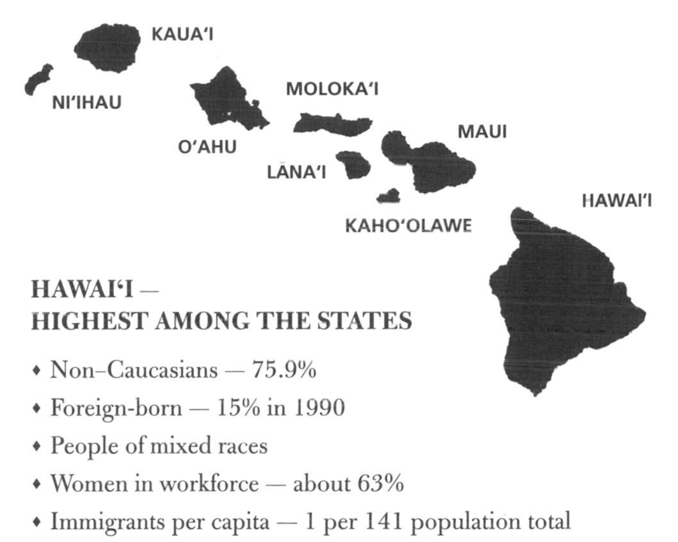

HAWAI'I — HIGHEST AMONG THE STATES

- Non–Caucasians — 75.9%
- Foreign-born — 15% in 1990
- People of mixed races
- Women in workforce — about 63%
- Immigrants per capita — 1 per 141 population total
- People under 65 (except Alaska 97.7%) — 89%
- People living longer — highest life expectancy (years) — males 75, females 80, average 77.5. Males: Chinese 78.4; Japanese 77.7; Filipinos 77.3; Caucasians 74.2; Hawaiians 70.9. Females: Chinese 81.7; Japanese 81.5; Filipinos 81; Caucasians 79.1; Hawaiians 76.
- Married couples living with others — because of Hawai'i's lowest percentage of home ownership

RELIGIONS

Denominations

Denomination	Number
Roman Catholic	215,000
Buddhist (All sects)	100,000
Mormon	56,000
United Church of Christ	19,000
Southern Baptist Convention	17,000
Episcopalian	10,000
United Methodist	7,000
Lutheran	6,000
Jewish	7,000

Dates established in Hawai'i

Congregationalist	1820
Roman Catholic	1827
Mormon	1850
Chinese Buddhist, Confucianist, Taoist	1852
Methodist	1854
Anglicans	1862
Lutherans	1883
Japanese Buddhist	1885
Seventh Day Adventist	1885
Salvation Army	1894
Christian Scientist	1902
Northern Baptist	1930
Southern Baptist	1940
Jewish Synagogue	1950
Unitarian	1953

❃ Precious Land ❃

4.1 MILLION ACRES

cropland	347,000 acres
grazing land	923,000 acres
forests	1,419,000 acres
urban and built-up	157,000 acres
misc./non-farmland	852,000 acres

WHO OWNS THE LAND?

- State and Counties — 29.8%
- Federal — 8.4%
- Private land owners — 61.8%. Six land owners account for 24% — Richard S. Smart Estate, Dole Food Co., Samuel Damon Estate, Alexander & Baldwin, C. Brewer & Co. and the Estate of James Campbell.
- Bishop Estate, the largest private land owner, holds about 10%. These are royal lands inherited by Princess Bernice Pauahi Bishop, last of the Kamehameha line. 375,000 acres were put into a foundation at her death in 1884 — then valued at $300,000 — in 1993 worth about $1.57 bil lion — profits from land use and leases provide funds for Kamehameha Schools.
- New land formed by lava flows belongs to the state, not to abutting property owners. So ruled the Hawaiʻi Supreme Court in 1977.

❃ Agriculture❃

Sugar — 70,000 acres on Maui and Kaua'i — yielding about 340,000 tons of raw sugar (2002)

- One ton of water needed to make a pound of sugar — irrigation costs about $50 million for about half the crops — rest depends on rainfall
- Crops average about 11 lbs. of raw sugar per acre
- No insecticides used — biological control of 11 major insect enemies
- Weed control by spray — hand, truck, airplane
- Rats cause $2 to $4 million loss annually — diminished by trapping and poisoning
- Production — over a million tons a year
- Most of the raw sugar refined by California and Hawai'i Sugar Co. (C and H), Crockett, Calif.

Pineapple — production about 320,000 tons, farm value of about $100.6 million (2002)

Papaya — chiefly on Hawai'i — about 55 million lbs. produced annually (2001)

Macadamia nuts — 18,000 acres, mostly on Hawai'i Island, producing 52 million pounds, farm value of about $29.6 million (2003)

Coffee — only commercial coffee grown in U.S. — 6,200 acres producing 8.5 million lbs. — value $19.6 million (2003)

Anthurium — 60 farms sold about 756,000 dozen — value $4.9 million (2002)

Livestock — over $64,815,000 worth produced a year (2001) — Parker Ranch on Hawai'i about 325,000 acres — largest Hereford cattle ranch in the world — largest privately owned (King Ranch in Texas run by a corporation)

❃ Cost of Living ❃

- High import costs, need for larger inventories, lack of land for housing, complex building permit procedures and code regulations, and high cost and level of government services make Hawai'i an expensive place to live
- Honolulu is the 2nd most expensive city in U.S., next to Anchorage, Alaska
- Housing costs 30% higher than on U.S. mainland — median home value on O'ahu in 1992 — $230,000.
- Land costs over 40% of total property value — national average about 20%
- Taxes — 5th highest after Alaska, New York, Wyoming, California — 3rd highest income tax above $10,000 level after Minnesota and Massachusetts; average property tax bills from $274 on O'ahu, $317 on Maui, $363 on Kaua'i to $377 on Hawai'i
- Intermediate-income family budget for four highest in U.S. — $31,893, or 26% higher than for average U.S. urban family.

Visiting Hawai'i

- Mild, even, warm temperature
- Green-covered grandeur of mountain slopes
- Abounding displays of beautiful flowers
- Physical wonders — mountains, canyons, cliffs, valleys, volcanoes
- Ocean shoreline panoramas
- Comfort of simple, colorful, light clothing
- Outdoor life — sightseeing, swimming, sunning on the beach, sports
- Interesting, exotic mixture of people
- Hawaiian entertainment — music and hula
- Food sensations — fruits, nuts, Asian and other national dishes
- Island-hopping — each with different attractions

❃ How Far from Home ❃ (or Someplace Else)?

HONOLULU TO:	MILES
San Francisco	2,297
Los Angeles	2,557
Portland	2,595
Seattle	2,679
Vancouver, B.C.	2,709
Anchorage	2,782
Guam	3,806
Tokyo	3,847
Chicago	4,179
Auckland, N.Z.	4,393
Washington, D.C.	4,829
Miami	4,856
New York	4,959
Sydney	5,070
Manila	5,293
Hong Kong	5,541

❋ Weather? Almost Perfect ❋

- How's the weather here? — As they say, "Sometimes same, sometimes little bit different."
- Sunny skies, balmy breezes, gentle surf — expect these. Be happy if it is just like that.
- Severe storms seldom — latest one, January 1980 — more than $20 million damage
- Hurricanes generally pass by — Dot hit Kaua'i, August 1959 — Iwa hit Kaua'i and O'ahu November 23, 1982, $234 million damage — Iniki hit Kaua'i and O'ahu September 1992, almost $2 billion damage
- Rainfall records — Wai'ale'ale, Kaua'i, "wettest spot on earth," has recorded over 600 inches/year — heaviest, 38 inches, Kīlauea Plantation, Kaua'i, 1956 — highest record by National Weather Service for 24-hour period, Hilo, Feb. 1979, 22.3 inches — most in one month, Pu'ukukui, Maui, 107 inches, March 1942
- Tidal waves — most destructive of Hawai'i's disasters — at least 358 lives lost in six — worst was April 1, 1946, 159 killed, 1,300 homes destroyed, $25 million damage, mostly Hilo, Hawai'i — again May 23, 1960, 61 killed, heavy damage to business section

• Earthquakes — worst in 1860s — biggest April 22, 1868, 81 killed, mostly in tidal waves and mud slides. Hawai'i had more than a quarter of all (404) quakes felt in the U.S. in 1982, 137.

❃ Favorite Attractions ❃

	Attendance in 2001
1. National Memorial Cemetery of the Pacific (1997)	5,000,000
2. Polynesian Cultural Center	758,314
3. U.S.S. *Arizona* Memorial	1,443,956
4. Hawai'i Volcanoes National Park	2,631,649
5. Sea Life Park (1999)	356,123

OTHER SPECIAL ATTRACTIONS

Waikīkī Beach	9,259,938
Hanauma Bay	1,526,835
Bishop Museum	410,565
Foster Botanical Garden (1999)	48,434
Lyman Memorial House Museum, Hilo	18,101
Volcano eruptions — if you're lucky!	

SOME BEAUTY SPOTS

Haleakalā Crater, Maui

Hawai'i Volcanoes National Park, Hawai'i

Hanalei Valley, Kaua'i

Pu'uhonua o Hōnaunau (City of Refuge) National Park, Hawai'i

Kīlauea Lighthouse, Kaua'i

Hāna, Maui

Kalaupapa, Moloka'i

Nāpili, Maui

Pali Lookout, O'ahu

Puna, Hawai'i

Photo: Douglas Peebles

❃ Hawaiian Holidays and Celebrations ❃

Prince Kūhiō Day — March 26, honoring birthday of Prince Jonah Kūhiō Kalaniana'ole, nephew of Queen Lili'uokalani and Republican delegate to Congress in 1902–1922

Lei Day — May 1, Hawai'i's pageantry version of May Day

Kamehameha Day — June 11, honoring founder of Kingdom of Hawai'i

Admission Day — 3rd Friday in August, commemorating Hawai'i's admission to the Union, August 21, 1959

Bon Dances — Japanese ceremonials — July and August

Aloha Week — a different week for each island — Mid-October to mid-November — royal processions and pageantry

Merrie Monarch Festival — Hilo in April — week-long festivities and popular hula contests attract dancers and spectators from all islands

❃ None Here! ❃
Happy Omissions

- Snakes
- Rabies — strict quarantine on incoming animals
- Cholera, malaria, small pox, yellow fever
- Billboards to spoil your view
- Hurricanes seldom

ALSO TO BE MISSED

- Grass skirts — hula skirts have ti leaves — Hawaiian women wore tapa skirts (pa'u)
- Hummingbirds — cross-pollination of pineapple blossoms would develop unwanted seeds in fruit

❃ Free Honolulu Entertainment ❃

Changing of the Guard — King's Village, everyday, 6:15 p.m.

Royal Hawaiian Band concerts — Call for venue, dates and times. Information: 922-5331

❃ Come Swim Hawai'i ❃ — But Don't Swim at Isolated Beaches!

Be wary, talk to other swimmers or a lifeguard to learn local conditions. Our Pacific Ocean injures, cripples, or kills dozens of Hawai'i residents and visitors every year. With hundreds of miles of coastline, Hawai'i suffers the poorest record in water safety in the U.S. So, be informed and careful — avoid being the victim of one of the many drownings, near-drownings, broken necks, or surfing and scuba diving injuries.

Beaches — besides sometimes overcrowded Waikīkī, try Kahana Bay and Ka'a'awa Beach Park, Kailua Beach, Bellows Beach (Friday noon to Sunday midnight), Hanauma Bay and Mā'ili Beach Park. Only expert surfers at Sunset Beach, 'Ehukai, and Hale'iwa Beach Parks (last two calmer and safer in summer)

Dangerous at Sandy Beach, Koko Head Beach Park, Waimea Bay — most dangerous on north and west shores

❃ Music of the Heart ❃

King David Kalākaua — words for national anthem, "Hawai'i Pono'ī" — also "Koni Au," Hawaiian drinking song

Queen Lili'uokalani — "Aloha Oe" — also "Hawaiian National Anthem," 1866, sung for some 20 years

Princess Likelike — " 'Āina-Hau"

Prince Leleihoku — "Kaua I Ka Huahua'i," love song familiar now as "Hawaiian War Chant"

Rev. Lorenzo Lyons — "Hawai'i Aloha," a favorite mission ary hymn

Capt. Henry Berger — leader of Royal Hawaiian Band from 1872 — arranged many songs, including "Hawai'i Pono'i" and "Hilo March"

Charles E. King — collected hapa-haole songs (English with Hawaiian words and phrases), arranged and published over 200 songs, including "Song of the Islands" (2nd most popular) and "Kamehameha Waltz"

Harry Owens — "To You, Sweetheart, Aloha" and "Sweet Leilani," sung by Bing Crosby and won Academy Award, 1937

R. Alex Anderson — "Lovely Hula Hands," 1940, and "The Cockeyed Mayor of Kaunakakai"

Alfred Apaka — "Greatest voice Hawai'i ever produced" — theme song "Here in This Enchanted Place"

Tony Todaro — "Keep Your Eyes on Hands" and "Somewhere in Hawai'i" — sung by Apaka

Don Ho — "Biggest in the history of Hawaiian show business" — popularized "Tiny Bubbles"

Kui Lee — Chinese-Hawaiian — composed, played guitar, sang, chatted briskly in pidgin — popular in 1960s — wrote and sang "Lahainaluna," "I'll Remember You," "One Paddle, Two Paddle"

Danny Kaleikini — leader and master of ceremonies at today's Hawaiian shows — sings, chats, cracks jokes — Hawaiian, Chinese, Korean, Irish, and Italian origin

❋ Foods ❋
Dining Treats

HAWAIIAN FRESH FISH

ʻAhi — Allison or yellowfin tuna

Aku — bonito, smaller tuna

Mahimahi — light white fish, dolphin fish (not the porpoise which is also called dolphin)

Ono — wahoo (mackerel family), another delicious white fish

ʻŌpakapaka — pink snapper

ʻŌpelu — mackerel, scad

Ulua — pompano

Humuhumunukunukuāpuaʻa — trigger fish, more popular in song than for eating

HAWAIIAN KAUKAU — LŪʻAU

Pūpū — appetizer

ʻOpihi — raw shellfish, limpet

Laulau — pork and fish steamed in ti leaf

Lomilomi salmon — salad of salmon, tomatoes, onions, squeezed together

Limu — fresh raw seaweed

Chicken long rice — with long thin noodles

Kim chi — Korean pickled cabbage

Kālua pig — pork baked in imu (underground oven)

Poi — mashed taro root: "He who says he likes poi is either a Hawaiian or a liar"

Haupia — coconut pudding

TASTE TESTS — SPECIAL FOODS

Adzuki — small red beans cooked, sweetened, mashed as fillings

Bamboo shoots — for meat and noodle dishes

Bean sprouts — in many Oriental dishes

Breadfruit — steamed, boiled, fried, baked, or mashed, baked with coconut cream

Chinese peas — flat pods lightly cooked

Daikon — Oriental long radish

Dasheen — Japanese for taro

Gobo — Japanese burdock

Lily buds — in duck and pork dishes

Lotus root — in meat dishes

Lūʻau — taro leaves cooked with milk, coconut milk, or fat, sometimes with chicken or octopus — always served at a party spread — in 1950s, came to mean "feast"

Malasadas — Portuguese round doughnuts, no hole

Miso — fermented soybean, rice, and salt paste for soup

Nori — paper-thin sheets of matted seaweed to wrap around vinegared rice with fish and vegetables

Saimin — noodles in Japanese dishes

Sashimi — small slices of raw fish in soy sauce

Shoyu — soy sauce

Sukiyaki — thin-sliced beef with lightly cooked vegetables

Tempura — batter-dipped meat, deep-fried

Teriyaki — meat marinated in soy sauce, broiled

Tofu — soybean curd — used with soy sauce in Oriental dishes

Water chestnuts — crisp slices for Chinese meat and vegetable dishes

Yam bean root (chop sui potato) — Chinese stir-fry dishes

ISLAND TREATS

Crack seed - preserved, seasoned, chewy fruits with cracked seeds, whole seeds, or seedless - also candied squash or coconut — watermelon or pumpkin seeds, pine nuts — even dried, smelly cuttlefish, squid, scallops, abalone, or octopus

YOUR FORTUNE, ANYONE?

Chinese and Japanese restaurants buy 3,000 to 5,000 fortune cookies a month from the Hawai'i Candy Company.

❃ Special in Hawai'i ❃

DRESS STYLES

Muʻumuʻu — large, informal comfortable "Mother Hubbard" dress (missionary style)

Holokū — graceful formal gown with long train

Holomū — somewhat less formal — no train

Chinamuu (Pekemuu) — fitted lines, frogged neckline, side-slit skirt, butterfly sleeves

LIQUORS

ʻŌkolehao — made from ti root, first produced in 1790 — name means "iron bottom," from the large iron kettle it was made in — " ʻŌkole maluna" means "Bottoms up!"

Sake (sahkay) — Japanese rice liquor made here by Honolulu Brewery and Ice Company, started 1908 — first active sake brewery built outside Japan — only one in the U.S. and possibly only other one in the world (except perhaps in Brazil). By developing great production techniques, it is the only one making sake year round.

❋ Suggested Hawaiian Gifts ❋

Clothing — Aloha wear; blouses, skirts, swimsuits, dresses, mu'umu'us, shirts, hats

Jewelry — leis (seed, shell, nut), polished kukui nuts (natural, but some plastic), polished 'opihi shells, puka shells (many imported), olivine (mostly from mainland)

Coral — black (discovered by Maui Divers in 1958) — pink from salmon red to almost white — highest quality termed "Angelskin"

Creations — lauhala bags, purses, mats, hula skirts, hula instruments, paintings, lava-metal artwork

Woodcraft — bowls, salad sets, trays, carvings — woods: monkeypod (much imported), koa (Hawaiian mahogany, beautiful grains and color tints), milo (fine wood but rarer)

Memories — books, cards, slides, records

Produce — coconuts, macadamia nuts, Kona coffee, fresh pineapple

Flowers — orchids, anthurium — plants specially prepared and pre-inspected

❃ Taking Away Plants, Fruits, and Flowers ❃

- **No restrictions** — ripe coconut, pineapple, macadamia nuts, flowers — EXCEPT gardenias, jade, mauna loa, any of pea family
- **Must be fumigated** — avocado, banana, litchi, papaya — fumigated fruit available at airport and some dealers
- **Mango** — must be pitted, frozen, or cooked
- **No plants in soil**
- **Orchids** — shops carry pre-inspected plants
- **No citrus** — All items checked at Airport Agricultural Inspection

Photo: Douglas Peebles

❃ Language ❃

Standardized by missionaries in 1820s — only 12-letter alphabet — 5 vowels, 7 consonants: h, k, l, m, n, p, w

PRONUNCIATION — VOWELS

a — ah — as in hale (house) — hahlay

e — ay — as in kane (man) — kahnay

i — ee — as in ipo (sweetheart) — eepoh

o — oh — as in ono (good) — ohnoh

u — ue — as in pūpū (snack) — puepue

COMMON WORDS

Activities

hana — work

hui — club, organization

hukilau — group net fishing

kōkua — help

lomilomi — massage

Clothing

haori — Japanese coat

holokū — gown

lavalava — Samoan skirt

malo — loincloth

mu‘umu‘u — long, loose dress

pāpale — hat

pa‘u — sarong-type skirt

Conditions

ho‘omalimali — flattery, sweet talk

huhū — anger

pilikia — trouble

wikiwiki — fast, hurry

Descriptions

akamai — clever, smart

auwe — alas

nani — beautiful

nui — big

ono — good tasting

pau — done, finished

pupule — crazy

Directions

kona — leeward, south, south wind

makai — toward sea

mauka — toward mountain

People

ali'i — chiefs, royalty

haole — white person

kahuna — priest in old Hawai'i, expert practitioner

kama'āina — native-born or long-time resident

kane — man

keiki — child, little one

kupuna — grandparent, ancestor

malihini — stranger, foreigner

paniolo — cowboy

tūtū — grandmother

wahine — woman

People — Japanese

issei — first-generation Japanese immigrant

kibei — nisei educated in Japan

nisei — second generation in Hawai'i

sansei — third generation in Hawai'i

Religion

akua — god

amakua — family god

Kanaloa — god of deep sea

Kane — giver of life

Kū — main god

lani — heaven

Lono — god of agriculture

mana — spirit, power

Pele — goddess of volcano

Things

ʻaʻā — rough, clinkery lava

hale — house

hīmeni — missionary hymns

hula — a dance

imu — underground oven

kāhili — feather-decorated royal standard

kai — sea

lānai — porch

lau — leaf

lua — hole, depression, toilet

mele — ancient chant

pāhoehoe — smooth or ropey lava

pua — flower

puka — hole, opening

pūneʻe — couch

wai — water

Expressions

da kine (pidgin) — whachamacallit

Hauʻoli lā hānau — Happy Birthday

Hauoli Makahiki Hou — Happy New Year

Mele Kalikimaka — Merry Christmas

mahalo nui — Many thanks

Pehea ʻoe? — How are you?

Hula

Natural History

The Hawaiian Island chain is an archipelago stretching 1,600 miles from Kure atoll, 1,200 miles northwest of Honolulu, to the Island of Hawai'i. It is the longest chain of islands in the world

City and County of Honolulu includes 132 islands and islets northwest of Kaua'i, making it the longest such land unit in the U.S.

Origin — volcanic action from a long fissure opening along the floor of the Pacific — Kure built up first above the surface of the sea — then came Midway Islands — then other atolls and small islands forming along the rift to the southwest

Age — started about 25 million years ago — continues with eruptions on Island of Hawai'i

❋ Those Impressive Islands — The Five Main Ones ❋

Glimpses of Hawai'i, Maui, and Moloka'i often may be caught from left side of plane on a trip from the mainland to Honolulu

Hawai'i — largest, greatest elevation, farthest east and south — youngest (less than a million years — still building up by volcanic action)

Maui 2nd largest — 2nd youngest — perhaps a half million years older than Hawai'i

Moloka'i — 5th in size, next older (but just a few hundred thousand years more)

O'ahu — 3rd largest — most populated — still older (a million or so years more)

Kaua'i — 4th largest — oldest (up to 5.6 million years)

❃ Big Island's Biggest ❃

MARVELOUS MAUNA KEA

- Tallest mountain in the world — measured from base 18,000 feet under sea — 29,400 to 30,000 feet high (Everest 29,028) — 13,796 above sea level
- Summit covered by icecap down to 11,000-foot level or below during Ice Age about 30,000 years ago
- Extinct volcano for 4,000 to 10,000 years
- Highest lake in the U.S. — Lake Waiau 13,020 feet high — 12,000 years old
- Largest adz quarry in Polynesia — best quality basalt rock for adzes to carve canoes, house posts, tikis
- Snow-covered for skiing in winter — glaciers in ancient geologic age
- Clearest air — highest astronomical observatories (thirteen) in world — biggest such complex

MIGHTY MAUNA LOA

- Most massive mountain in the world — 10,000 cubic miles — 60 miles long, 30 wide — active volcano
- World's largest and deepest well — 4,300 feet deep, 85 feet below sea level, 12 inches in diameter — drilled November 1982 to February 1983

MAUNA LOA — 1950 ERUPTION

- Heaviest destruction in 150 years
- 7 major rivers of lava gushed down from west rift zone
- Flowed for 23 days
- 35 square miles covered
- 514 million cubic yards of lava added on land — more than 100 million dumped into sea
- 125 had to flee from homes — but no lives lost
- 3 great flows crossed Belt Road: Ka'apuna Flow — largest, farthest south, wiped out houses and new motel with restaurant and two cottages; Ka'ohe Flow — middle one, destroyed Magoon Ranch house and pasture land; Honokua Flow — northern, covered mauka Ho'okena village, post office, service station, church, burial grounds under 30 ft. of lava

MAUNA LOA — 1984 ERUPTION

- Starting March 25, 13,000 feet up Mauna Loa, streams of lava as great as 24 million cubic meters a day poured down the east flank. The eruption lasted 22 days and threatened Hilo by coming within just 4 miles of the city.

❃ Mauna Loa — Major Recent Eruptions ❃

Date		Location	Cu. Meters
1952	June–Nov.	Halemaʻumaʻu	49,000,000
1954	June–July	Halemaʻumaʻu	6,500,000
1955	Feb,–May	Puna	92,000,000
1959	Nov.–Dec.	Kīlauea Iki	39,000,000
1960	Jan.–Feb.	Puna, Kapoho	119,000,000
1961	Feb and Mar.	Halemaʻumaʻu	515,000
	July	Halemaʻumaʻu	13,200,000
	Sept.	Puna	2,500,000
1962	Dec.	ʻĀloʻi crater	326,000
1963	Aug.	ʻAlae crater	840,000
	Oct.	Nāpau, Kalalua	7,700,000
1965	Mar.	Makaopuhi to Kalalua	17,600,000
	Dec.	ʻĀloʻi crater	840,000
1967/8	Nov.–July	Halemaʻumaʻu	84,000,000
1968	Oct.	West of Kalalua	7,000,000

1969	Feb.	ʻĀloʻi to Puʻu Kamoamoa	17,000,000
	Mar.-Oct.	Mauna Ulu	185,000,000
1971	Aug.	Caldera floor	9,500,000
	Sept.	Halemaʻumaʻu and SW	8,000,000
1972	Feb.	Maunaulu and ʻAlae	72,000,000
1974	July	Kīlauea	14,000,000
	Sept.	Kīlauea, Halemaʻumaʻu	8,000,000
	Dec.	Southwest rift	14,000,000
1975	Nov.	Kīlauea, Halemaʻumaʻu	250,000
1977	Sept.	Puna	45,000,000
1979	Nov.	Kīlauea, Pauahi	700,000
1982	Apr.	Caldera	500,000
	Sept.	Caldera	3-4,000,000
1983	Jan.	Kīlauea (phase 48 began July 1986, has added almost 400 acres of new land, continuing March 1994	
1995	Dec.	Kīlauea still in progress; 53 different eruptions have destroyed 181 housing units and added 540 acres to the land	
1998	Mar.	Kīlauea still erupting. The eruption is called "Puʻu ʻoʻo Kupaianaha". It has added 570 acres to the land	

❃ Birds ❃

- More birds have become extinct in Hawai'i than in any other area of the world — 26 species lost, 27 more are threatened by changes in natural habitats, forest destruction, cats and mongooses, and man.
- Largest bird sanctuary in the world — Hawaiian Islands National Wildlife Refuge on the leeward islands northwest of Kaua'i, is a haven for vast colonies of seabirds.

INTRODUCED SPECIES

Brazilian cardinal — on O'ahu — red head, bluish-gray back, white below

California quail

Cardinal — from about 1929

Chukar — from Asia, 1923

Dove — small barred from Malaysia, 1922; large spotted, before 1900

English sparrow — in coastal areas before 1870

House finch — from before 1870

Mynah — from India, 1865

Pheasant — from China, about 1865

Ricebird — from about 1865

Skylark — on Hawai'i, Maui, O'ahu

White-eye — from Japan, 1929

NATIVE BIRDS

Nēnē — Hawai'i state bird — native wild goose that almost became extinct. Flocks of 25,000 or more roamed mountain slopes of Maui and Hawai'i, then dwindled to fewer than 50 by 1940, killed off by hunters and predators — mongooses, rats, wild cats and dogs, and people. Perhaps descended from Canadian goose — feet adapted for walking over rough lava. Restoration project of propagation started in 1954. Over 1,750 have been released now, some on Maui, but mostly on Hawai'i.

Hawaiian hawk ('Io) — Hawai'i Island only

Short-eared owl (Pueo) — all main islands

White-tailed tropicbird — March–October — especially Kaua'i valleys and Kīlauea crater

Many other rarer species in higher forested areas

MIGRATORY VISITORS

Gull, Plover, Sandpiper, Sooty shearwater, Teal

❃ Animals ❃

No snakes! — banned, but some rarely smuggled in, as some garter snakes and even a python — occasional sea snakes

Feral domestic animals — released in 19th century — cattle, goats, pigs, sheep — now game for hunters — also axis deer on Moloka'i

Dogs — brought here by Polynesians for meat

Rats — may have come with the Polynesians, or from visiting Western ships — now a plague, especially for sugarcane growers

Mongoose — imported from Jamaica in 1883 to kill rats in sugarcane — but they sleep at night when rats are out doing their damage

Bats — only native warm-blooded animal in Hawai'i — this species considered rarest in world

❃ Native Plants ❃

Hawai'i has the highest percentage of endemic (found nowhere else) plants in the world: 96% here before Polynesians came, 4% indigenous to other Pacific islands. 2,500 grow only in remote areas now. Half of U.S.'s threatened and endangered plants grow in Hawaiian Islands, only 2% of the country's land surface. Decline is due to feral animals — wild pigs, goats, sheep, cats, dogs — and uncontrolled exotic plants — bamboo, ginger, guava, creeping passion fruit, which smoother native flora. The silversword is unique to Hawai'i and is found only on Haleakalā, Maui, and on Mauna Kea and Mauna Loa on Hawai'i Island. Koa and 'ōhi'a trees (see Special Trees) are also significant native Hawaiian plants.

Photo: Douglas Peebles

❋ Special Trees ❋
Native and Introduced

Autograph tree (Copey or Scotch attorney) — beach areas — write on its hard, thick round leaves

Banyan — widespreading, with roots that hang from its branches

Barringtonia (Hutu) — grated seeds a poison to stun fish

Calabash tree — gourds for hula rattles

Chinaberry (Pride of India) — wood for hula instruments — chiefly on Hawai'i and Moloka'i

Christmas berry — heavy brushy growth along roads — red berry clusters for Christmas decorations

Coconut — for food and drink and many uses of wood — leaves for roofing, screens, baskets, coverings, matting blossoms for liquor — trimming trees is big business — 40,000 trees with 1 1/2 million nuts a year — most go to city dumps, since there is no market here, yet some are import ed from the South Pacific

Eucalyptus — from Australia — fastest growing — lumber, paper pulp, oil for medicines, solvents — perfumes from leaves — flowers for nectar for honey bees — trees used as ornamentals and windbreaks — prevent soil erosion

Kamani — sacred Polynesian tree — oil from nuts for lamps, medicines, waterproofing, paint, lacquer

Kamani, false — large leaves turn red and yellow — nuts shape and taste of almonds

Kiawe (Algaroba, Mesquite) — seeds brought to Hawai'i by Catholic priests from France — grows in dry coastal areas — yellow pods for cattle fodder — ideal wood for imu and charcoal — blossoms good source of honey

Koa (Hawaiian mahogany) — most valuable forest tree — one of largest and most prized hardwoods — for ocean-going canoes, surfboards, furniture, 'ukuleles, carvings

Kou — evergreen seaside tree — rarest wood — orange flowers — small, round, white edible fruit — wood for native dishes, since it has no taste of its own

Kukui (Candlenut) — nuts polished as ornaments and leis — oil once exported for use in paints — nuts used as laxative and baby food

Monkeypod — large, common, umbrella shaped tree — wood for furniture and carvings

Norfolk Island pine — beautiful, symmetrical evergreen up to 150 ft. — excellent Christmas tree — brought here to grow masts for sailing ships — but steamships in use before trees were tall enough

ʻŌhiʻa (Hawaiian black walnut) — blossoms called lehua — nectar for birds and honey — hard reddish wood — ideal for posts, flooring, furniture, firewood, tikis

ʻOpiuma — name from opium-like black seeds used for leis — small white brushlike flowers become red twisted pods in spring — wood for lumber, dye, gum from bark

Palms — 1,500 species: in Hawaiʻi, coconut, date, fan, queen, and royal varieties

Paper bark — name from peeling layers of birchlike bark — used for thatching — small white brushlike blossoms — leaf oil for medicines — tree good for erosion control

Sandalwood — practically extinct now — kings had men strip forests for Chinese trade — scented wood for incense, perfumes, chests, furniture

Tree fern (Hāpuʻu) — rain forest growth — young coiled fronds cooked as vegetables — soft reddish-brown fiber (pulu) used to check bleeding and for embalming — was exported for pillows and mattresses in mid-1800s — trees give shade for anthurium — fibrous wood serves as base material for rooting orchids

❋ Polynesian Imported Plants ❋
Their Mainstays of Life

Bamboo — one of man's most useful plants — for boat parts, containers, dishes, fishing equipment, food, furniture, hats, implements, mats, musical instruments — fastest growing recorded at 47.6 inches in 24 hours — 1,250 species — tallest 125 feet — dies after flowering at 50 to 100 years old.

Banana — matures in 14 months — only one bunch per tree — new trees from suckers around base

Breadfruit — ripens October to March — weighs up to 10 lbs. — eaten baked, boiled, broiled, or glazed

Coconut — about 5 lbs. — best drink is "water" from green ones — milk made by squeezing grated meat from young nut through cloth

Gourds — provide containers, musical instruments

Hau — true hibiscus — yellow flower changing to apricot color, then dark red

Kukui — oil for stone dish lamps — candles of nuts strung on coconut fibers — torches of nuts stuffed in bamboo — bark to dye tapa, fish nets — baby food of ground roasted nuts with poi — mouthwash from sap — oil from green nuts for aching muscles — laxative from 1-3 green nuts

Lauhala (Hala, Pandanus, Screw pine) — also called "walking trees," because roots spread out and down from trunk — leaves (lau) for thatch, mats, baskets, purses, sandals, fans — fruit like pineapple in shape only — not eaten

Lipstick plant — bright yellow dye from scarlet seeds

Milo — small yellow hibiscus-like flowers — wood for food bowls because it has little flavor

Paper mulberry (Wauke) — bark for tapa cloth

Sugarcane — energy source for long voyages

Taro (Kalo) — large leaf — root cooked as food and to make poi

Ti — green leaf variety sacred — to keep away evil spirits from temple and home — good luck symbol — root steamed as food — also used to make liquor — as food, helped prevent scurvy for sailors — leaves for laulaus, hula skirts, wrappers, thatch, table decorations

Sweet potatoes, yams, turmeric, and **wild ginger** were also brought to Hawai'i by the Polynesians.

❃ Fruits ❃

Avocado — about 100 varieties bearing different times give year-round supply — vary in taste, color, shape, size, skin — more than a million lbs. yearly, mostly from the island of Hawaiʻi — can't be exported

Banana — over 70 species, 300 varieties — some for cooking — favorites: dwarf Chinese (Cavendish), Williams hybrid, bluefield (from Bluefield, Nicaragua) — nearly half million lbs. a month

Berries — ʻākala (native raspberry), blackberry, ʻōhelo, pohā (ground cherry), pōpolo, thimbleberry

Citrus — calamondin, citron, grapefruit, kumquat, lemon, lime, orange, pomelo, tangelo, tangerine

Guava — yellow — good for juice, jelly, desserts — plants a pest when spreading wild

Litchi (Laichi, Lychee) — not a nut — small fruit with thin red shell — sweet juicy white flesh

Macadamia — delectable hardshell nuts — holly-like leaves — imported from Queensland, Australia, 1892

Mango — one of the finest tasting fruits in the world — ripens March to October — longest life of any fruit tree — more people in the world eat mangos than eat apples — favorite varieties: Haden and Pirie

Mountain apple — not an apple — round to bell-shape in white, pink, and red shades — applelike flesh but juicier with delicate flavor

Papaya — 45 species — orange or red flesh — up to 8 lbs. — 3 kinds of trees — male (no edible fruit), female (round fruit), bisexual (self-pollinating) grows and matures in a year — favorite commercial variety: Solo — small, solid, from Jamaica, 1911, bears year round — twice vitamin C of orange — also vitamin A and pectin — plant's milky fluid for meat tenderizers, papain

Passion fruit (Liliko'i) — yellow on long vine — for juice, jelly, desserts — in flower, 10 sepals and petals for 10 aposteles at Crucifixion — fringed crown for crown of thorns — 5 stamens for 5 wounds — styles for 3 nails — tendrils for scourges — leaves for hands of persecutors — Hawaiian name from Liliko'i Gulch, Maui

Pineapple — single fruit to plant, ripens in 20 to 24 months — 2nd most important agricultural product

Star apple — named for shape — trees grown more for foliage than for edible fruit

❃ Flowering Trees ❃

African tulip — large, red-orange flowers — also new golden variety

Angel's trumpet — small tree — large white hanging flowers

Be still (yellow oleander) — small tree with small trumpet-shaped flowers — not an oleander, but similar leaves

Bottle brush — small tree with drooping red flowers like its name

Buttercup — small tree with rich yellow flowers like its name

Christmas berry — bushlike with masses of red berries

Gold tree (Primavera) — tall tree with masses of golden tubular blossoms when leafless

Jacaranda — bunches of soft lavender-blue blossoms, usually in spring

Octopus (Umbrella) — tall with long arms with rows of small, dark red flowers like octopus suckers

ʻŌhiʻa lehua — red pompom blossoms

Orchid tree (Bauhinia) — orchidlike flowers — St. Thomas with white or pink flowers

Plumeria (Frangipani) — many varieties in white, yellow, pink, red — Singapore variety: white flowers, rounded dark evergreen leaves

Poinciana, royal (Flamboyant) — dome-shaped with orange or red-orange flowers late in spring or in summer

Potato tree — purple flowers that fade lighter, almost to white — blooms year round

Sausage tree — deep red hanging flowers that form into long sausage-shaped dangling pods

Shower trees — Coral: pink — blooms March–May; Pink and White: May–June; Golden: yellow hanging flower clusters — summer–fall; Rainbow: combinations of colors — summer–fall

Silk oak (Silver oak) — tall with dark yellow feathery flowers — wood like that of oak

Tigers claw (Indian coral, Wiliwili haole) — bright red flowers at tips of branches after leaves drop — January–February

❃ Flowering Shrubs ❃

Aloe (Red hot poker) — cactuslike with stick-up stem of orange-red small flowers

Beefsteak — bright red leaves — also a yellow variety

Candlebush — tipped with cylindrical yellow blossoms

Chenile plant — dangling thin dark red tails

Croton — mix-colored leaves of many varieties

Crown flower (Giant milkweed) — white or pale lavender flowers with small crown in center — used for leis

Dwarf poinciana — clusters of orange-red or yellow blossoms

Gardenia — blooms April–September, especially June

Hibiscus — more than 5,000 varieties of hybrids developed here

'Ilima — small, hibiscus-shaped yellow-orange blossoms — formerly reserved for royalty

Ixora — large red ball of small blossoms

Lehua haole — small leaves, fluffy red pompom flowers like native lehua

Lipstick plant — dainty pale orchid-pink flower — dark red pointed pods turn ruddy brown — used in dry arrangements — dyes from pods, seed, skin, and pulp formerly used to color margarine and cheese — stimulant in mashed seed pulp was used to excite bulls for bull fights

Oleander — clusters of flowers — single or double — various tones, white to red

Pīkake (Arabian jasmine) — for leis, flavoring tea — Hawaiian name because Princess Kaiulani was fond of jasmine and peacocks

Plumbago — pale blue blossoms for ground cover or hedge

Poinsettia — rich red singles and doubles — also light pink and creamy yellowish — showy masses on banks and as hedges make brilliant roadside attractions in winter

Scrambled eggs (Kalamona) — clusters of bright yellow flowers — also grows wild as a vine

Tiare (Tahitian gardenia) — single starlike white flowers — very fragrant — waxen green leaves

❃ Flowers on the Vine ❃

Bougainvillea — over 100 varieties of leaf colors — single and double — first planting here was purple for Queen Emma, 1875; plant now oldest in Hawai'i — 3 feet across

Cup of gold — large, 9-inch blossom, light yellow — scent like that of ripe apricot

Jade vine — long hanging clusters of bluish jade-green claw-like flowers — January–April — also a rich orange-red variety

Orange trumpet (Firecracker vine, Huapala) — masses of long, narrow orange blossoms — January–April

Periwinkle — white or pink flowers on low-growing, spreading plants

Sandpaper vine (Petrea) — cascading light lavender-blue flowers — year round but best in spring

Stephanotis — the wedding blossom of pure white clusters with penetrating fragrance

Thunbergia — large and small varieties in white or lavender-blue

Yellow alamanda — large rich-yellow blossoms on vine tips — single or double

❃ Tropical Flowers ❃

Anthurium (Flamingo flower) — waxlike — some 500 varieties — white to red, some orange and green — last 3 weeks

Bird of paradise — orange and blue — like brilliant bird's head

Gingers — about 1,300 species — 47 genera — bloom March to December

> **Blue** — purplish-blue upright spikes — but not a true ginger
>
> **Crepe (Malay)** — bell-shape, fringed white flowers
>
> **Kahili** — loose, erect yellow-red heads
>
> **Red** — rich red overlapping bracts, upright
>
> **Shell** — drooping clusters, shell-like — delicately shaded in white and yellow with red dashes
>
> **Torch** — largest — with red head like overlapping scales — also pink
>
> **White (Ginger lily)** — mothlike with delightful fragrance
>
> **Yellow** — mothlike but smaller than white — used for traditional leis

Heliconia — hanging and upright varieties with series of richly colored bracts and large leaves (of banana family)

Lobster claw — upright series of alternate pointed red bracts in clawlike form

Hanging — string of dark red pointed bracts, small yellow flowers protruding — also one with red keels edged with green and yellow

Pink and green — upright bracts, pinkish center bordered by light yellow and green

Night-blooming cereus — rich-scented white and yellow blossoms in evening on heavy cactuslike wall vine — June and October

Orchids — thousands of varieties

Cattleya — large blossoms in many colors, forms and combinations

Cymbidium — delicately tinted waxlike — long-lasting

Cypripedium — lady slipper type

Dendrobium — cane orchids — blossoms in sprays — variety of colors

Epidendrum — loose blossom head of bright little flowers — variety of colors

Miltonia — pansylike in pink, lavender, purple, and white

Oncidium — variety of forms — many like butterflies and insects — mostly bright yellow with brown markings

Phalaenopsis — moth orchids, so-named because of size and shape — very showy

Vanda — varies in size and color combinations of blue, brown, pink, red, white in dots, streaks, and veins

❃ Flowers by Color ❃

Red — Trees: African tulip, bottle brush, octopus, lehua, plumeria, rainbow shower, royal poinciana, sausage, tiger's claw. Shrubs: aloe, chenille, ginger, hibiscus, ixora, lehua haole, poinsettia. Vines: red jade. Tropicals: anthurium, heliconia

Pink — Trees: coral shower, monkeypod, plumeria, oleander, pink and white shower. Vines: congea, periwinkle

Yellow, Orange — Trees: be still, buttercup, gold tree, golden shower, kiawe, plumeria, silk oak. Shrubs: candlebush, dwarf poinciana, ginger, ilima, scrambled eggs. Vines: cup of gold, orange trumpet, woodrose, yellow alamanda. Tropical: bird of paradise

Blue, Lavender, Purple — Trees: jacaranda, orchid tree, potato tree. Shrubs: plumbago. Vines: jade vine, sandpaper vine, thunbergia

White — Trees: angel's trumpet, bamboo. Shrubs: crown flower, gardenia, pikake, spider lily, tiare. Vines: night blooming cereus, passion fruit, thunbergia

❋ Preserving Cut Flowers ❋

Anthurium — cut 1/2 inch off stem — immerse flower and stem in water (room temperature) 2 hours or more — every 5 days cut another 1/2 inch and soak again; do not refrigerate — keeps 2 to 4 weeks

Bird of paradise — to bring out extra flowers, soak flower heads 20 minutes — insert thumb through slit on upper side — gently lift out flower — remove white membrane and cut off — keeps 1 to 2 weeks

Heliconia — sponge with soap suds to remove white powder — rinse in fresh water — do not soak — keeps 1 to 2 weeks

Red ginger — soak stem and flower 1/2 hour every 3 days — keeps 2 to 3 weeks

Shell ginger — soak 10 minutes — remove natural sheath around flowers — keeps about a week

❃ Hawaiian Medicinal Plants ❃

Aloe — excellent for swelling, burns, sunburns — used in some prepared medicines

'Ape *(Ahpay)* — used as a burn cure — leaves for headaches or neuralgia

Breadfruit ('Ulu) — milky sap for cuts and cracked skin

Hala (Pandanus) — for tumors — flower for constipation

Herbaca — tea served as birth control

Hinahina — leaves brewed into tea for diabetes

Kukui (Candlenut) — used for thrush, internal disease, asthma, tuberculosis — flower for diarrhea

Laukahi — leaves for debility and diabetes

Noni — for swelling, thrush, diabetes, tumor, dizziness, high blood pressure — juice of fruit for diarrhea, typhoid, or paratyphoid

❃ Watch Out! Poisonous Plants! ❃

Azalea — all parts

Be still (Yellow oleander) — all parts

Bird of paradise — seed pods

Castor bean — all parts, especially seeds

Coral plant — seeds

Crown flower — milky juice

Lantana — berries

Oleander — all parts

Pencil plant — all parts

Poinsettia — leaves, stem, sap

❃ Plant Names — Odd Facts ❃

Blue ginger — purple — not ginger
California pepper tree — from Mexico
Cherry — many different kinds in different plant groups
Hawaiian Christmas berry — native of Brazil
Mock orange — three unrelated kinds
Pīkake (Arabian jasmine) — native of India
Rubber trees — same name for three different plants

❋ The Outdoor Circle Helps Beautify Hawai'i ❋

- Organization formed in 1911 to promote the beautification of Hawai'i
- Donated and planted thousands of trees and ornamental shrubs along streets and highways
- Promoted hibiscus as official state flower in 1923 — planted 1,000 red- and yellow-flowered hibiscus bushes on grounds of new State Capitol
- Pressured banishment of billboards completely by 1927
- Helped preserve Diamond Head as first State Monument in 1965

History

HAWAI'I HAS THE OLDEST:

- **American school west of Rocky Mountains** — Lahaina Luna, Maui, founded 1831
- **Bank** — First Hawaiian Bank, opened 1858 as Bishop & Co.
- **Churches** — Pūko'o, Moloka'i, built 1835; first established Hawaiian Christian church, Moku'aikaua, Kailua-Kona, founded 1820, present building 1836; in Honolulu, KawaiaHa'o, completed 1842
- **Frame house** — Mission House, Honolulu — timbers from Boston, erected 1841
- **Newspaper west of Rocky Mountains** — Sandwich Island Gazette, 1836–1839
- **Residence still in use** — Washington Place, built 1846 — now governor's mansion, Honolulu
- **State health dept. in U.S.** — established 1850, 19 years before the first one on the mainland (Massachusetts, 1869)
- **U.S. company west of Rocky Mountains** — C. Brewer & Co., 1826

❃ High Points of Hawaiian History ❃

ca. 300–500 A.D.	Marquesan settlers
ca. 1095–1300	Tahitian settlers
1778	Capt. Cook encounters the Hawaiian Islands, anchoring off Kaua'i; killed the following year at Kealakekua Bay, Hawai'i
1782	Kamehameha king of Hawai'i Island
1795	Kamehameha I (ca. 1758–1819) conquers all islands except Kaua'i
1810	Kaua'i ceded to Kamehameha I
1819	Kamehameha I dies at Kailua-Kona; son, Liholiho (1797–1824), assumes the throne as Kamehameha II and rules with regent Queen Ka'ahumanu
1820	First American Protestant missionaries arrive from Boston
1824	Kauikeaouli (1814–1854), son of Kamehameha I, becomes Kamehameha III on death of Liholiho. Queen Kamamalu dies of measles in London.

1840	Kamehameha III creates Hawai'i's first written constitution
1842	U.S. recognizes kingdom
1845	Honolulu becomes capital; first legislature
1848	Great Māhele — dividing of land
1850	Foreigners allowed to own land
1852	First Chinese contract laborers arrive
1855	Kamehameha III dies. Kamehameha IV, Alexander Liholiho (1834–1863), nephew and adopted son of Kamehameha III, becomes sovereign
1860	King and Queen Emma found Queen's Hospital
1863	Kamehameha IV dies. Prince Lot Kamehameha (1830–1872), older brother of Alexander, ascends the throne as Kamehameha V.
1868	First Japanese laborers arrive
1873	William Charles Lunalilo (rules 1835–1874), descendant of a half-brother of Kamehameha I, becomes first elected king
1874	King Lunalilo dies. Prince David Kalākaua (1836–1891) elected over his rival, Queen Emma.

1878	First Portuguese contract laborers arrive from Madeira
1891	King Kalākaua dies, succeeded by his sister, as Queen Lili'uokalani (1838–1917)
1892	First pineapple cannery
1893	Revolution ends with Provisional Government
1894	Republic of Hawai'i
1898	Hawai'i becomes U.S. Territory
1900	First territorial government
1941	December 7, Japanese attack Pearl Harbor
1959	Hawai'i becomes 50th State. In the first state elections, 170,000 of 183,000 registered voters voted (93.6%) and elected 42 of Asian descent (mainland best all-time voting record, 77.4%).
1976	Voyaging canoe *Hōkūle'a* makes round-trip voyage to Tahiti and confirms the days of ancient Polynesian transpacific travel.
1993	'Onipa'a (stand fast) ceremonies held on the hundredth anniversary of the 1893 overthrow of the monarchy. President Bill Clinton signs a congressional resolution acknowledging the illegal overthrow of the Kingdom of Hawai'i in 1893.

✻ The First Hawaiians: Where Did They Come From? ✻

Different peoples from Southeast Asia gradually migrated south and east. As their navigational skills advanced, so did these seafaring people to settle the low islands of Micronesia, the more southern islands of Melanesia from the Solomons to Fiji, and finally the great Polynesian Triangle from New Zealand east to Easter Island and north to Hawai'i.

Scientific studies by the Bishop Museum of campsites at South Point on the island Hawai'i indicate that people from the Marquesas (northeast of Tahiti) were settling there about 750 A.D.. By about the year 1000, other arrivals from Tahiti and others of the Society Islands were populating the Hawaiian Islands.

❋ The First Europeans in Hawai'i ❋

Captain James Cook, on his third voyage, sailed north from the Society Islands heading toward America to seek the much-desired Northwest Passage. Though he sighted O'ahu in the Hawaiian chain first on January 18, 1778, adverse winds drove his ships westward, bringing him to land on western Kaua'i, near Waimea, on January 20.

Because Captain Cook served in the British navy, under the Earl of Sandwich, first lord of the admiralty, he honored the earl by giving these lands he had found the name Sandwich Islands. The word "sandwich" is also thought to have come from the earl's habit of eating such food. The name Sandwich Islands remained in use until about the 1850s

Photo: Hawai'i Sate Archive

❃ Captain Cook's Demise ❃

Photo: Hawai'i Sate Archive

Late in 1778, Captain Cook returned to winter in the Sandwich Islands, visiting Maui and finally settling in Kealakekua Bay, on the island of Hawaiʻi, January 16, 1779. By February 4, when Cook sailed off north, his ships refitted and supplied, the Hawaiians, by then bereft of much of their food and wearied by these unusual guests, felt much relieved.

Three days later a bad storm so damaged the foremast of the *Resolution* that the British ships had to return to the bay for repairs. The natives, now far less friendly, engaged in thefts and fights with the sailors. After the largest boat of the *Discovery* disappeared one night, Captain Cook followed his usual method and, on February 14, with a lieutenant and nine marines, went to take the high chief and hold him until the missing boat was returned.

But the chief's native guards held him back. A crowd began to gather, and it became more aroused and aggressive,

especially when news came that British men had fired upon and killed another chief in his double canoe. Cook started to withdraw. A club hit him. He turned and fired, ordering the marines to fire, too. Stabbed by an iron dagger, Cook fell face downward into the bay.

The boats fired into the melee. The Hawaiians retrieved many native bodies, dead or wounded, as well as those of Cook and four marines. Captain Clerke got part of Cook's body for burial in the bay, but other parts went to chiefs who had joined in the fight. The ships sailed out of the bay again on February 22 on their way back to England

❃ King Kamehameha I, the Great ❃

Kamehameha ("the lonely one") was the right man at the right time. He was a strong leader, brought up at the court of his uncle Kalaniʻōpuʻu, king of the island of Hawaiʻi, with whom he visited aboard Captain Cook's ship in 1778 and 1779 and learned of the modern power of gunfire.

After Kalaniʻōpuʻu's death in 1782, Kamehameha waged war against his rivals on Hawaiʻi at various intervals until 1790, defeating all but Keoua. By then, with an arsenal of modern

weapons and two former British sailors, John Young and Isaac Davis, to put the guns to helpful use, he conquered Maui and then Moloka'i. As he prepared to invade O'ahu, he had to return to Hawai'i to again battle the aggressive Keoua.

Seeking divine assistance, Kamehameha built for his war god the massive stone temple of Pu'ukoholā at Kawaihae. Then the ruling chiefs from Maui to Kaua'i came in a great fleet. Kamehameha defeated these invaders in a great battle off Waipi'o Valley. More divine help came when the volcano goddess Pele destroyed a third of Keoua's army with an explosive eruption of Kīlauea. Keoua was invited by Kamehameha to the dedication of the great temple at Kawaihae, and one of the chiefs there killed him as he stepped ashore.

In 1794 Kamehameha retook Maui and Moloka'i, and then O'ahu the next year, thus founding his kingdom with all except Kaua'i. High seas forced his fleet back in an attempt to attack Kaua'i in 1796. A fearful epidemic broke up invasion preparations in 1804. He had another fleet assembled

in 1810, but an American trader, Captain Nathan Winship, induced the Kaua'i king to sail with him to Honolulu, and Kamehameha there agreed that Kaua'i should be a tributary kingdom ruled by its king.

In 1812, Kamehameha retired to Kailua-Kona, ruling as a wise and understanding peaceful king until his death, May 8, 1819. No one since has been able to find where his royal bones were hidden. For Hawai'i, he had waged the war to end wars among the islands, bringing a divided people together into the modern world.

Three copies of the famous Kamehameha statue now stand in significant places: (1) Kapa'au, Kohala, Hawai'i — original casting in Florence, Italy, lost at sea near the Falkland Islands, later recovered and placed here, fulfilling a kahuna's prediction that the one ordered by King Kalākaua for Honolulu would come to Kohala, legendary birthplace of Kamehameha. (2) Honolulu, 'Iolani Palace Square — duplicate made after the original was lost. (3) National Statuary Hall, U.S. Capitol, Washington, D.C. — copy made in 1969 to represent the State of Hawai'i.

❋ The Hawaiian Flag ❋

Captain George Vancouver, a friend to Kamehameha I and the Hawaiian people, felt that the islands should be under the protection of Great Britain. With Kamehameha's consent, Vancouver hoisted the British flag over the royal house in 1794 to signify the islands a protectorate of his country. This, however, was never ratified by the British government, though foreign ships did recognize the British interests in the islands and the flag continued to fly over the developing kingdom.

It was Captain George Beckley, a patriotic Englishman, who designed the present flag and raised it in about 1816 over the fort he commanded in Honolulu. In the upper left-hand corner, he kept the British design of the three crosses of the patron saints of England, Scotland, and Ireland. For the kingdom, he added eight red, white, and blue stripes to represent the eight Hawaiian Islands.

❋ King Kamehameha II ❋

Photo: Hawai'i Sate Archive

Liholiho, as Kamehameha II, served with Kamehameha's favorite queen, Ka'ahumanu (who had been Liholiho's guardian) as joint ruler from 1819 to 1824. He helped break the kapu system of religion by eating with Ka'ahumanu and the queen mother. During his reign, the devastating sandalwood trade was carried on, whaling became important, and the first Christian missionaries arrived.

He and his favorite queen, Kamamalu, visited England in 1824 and died there in July from measles, lacking immunity to this foreign disease. A British warship commanded by Lord Byron carried the royal bodies back to Hawai'i.

❃ New England Missionaries Come to Hawai'i ❃

The strange life of Henry Obookiah from Hawai'i Island became the driving influence that sent New England missionaries to Hawai'i. Orphaned by the slaughter of his family, later studying to become a kahuna (native priest) at the temple at Kealakekua Bay, Henry swam out one day to a Yankee ship and accepted the captain's invitation to sail with him to New England. For ten years he worked on New England farms, attended schools, and gained an education and a love for Christianity. While completing his studies at the Foreign Missionary School at Cornwall, Connecticut, he succumbed to typhus fever.

The story of his valiant struggle and high hopes of returning to Hawai'i to take Christianity to his dear people stirred the aspirations of religious enthusiasts to carry out his eager ambitions. The Pioneer Company, consisting of two ministers, two teachers, a doctor, printer, and agriculturist, along with their wives, five children, and four native boys, sailed on the trading ship *Thaddeus* from Boston, October 23, 1819, and arrived at Kailua-Kona on April 4, 1820, and at Honolulu on April 19.

❃ Missionary Influence ❃

Photo: Hawai'i Sate Archive

Asa and Lucy Thurston

Whether you believe the missionaries had a good or bad effect on Hawai'i may depend on your social and religious inclinations and on the stories you use as evidence. The most damning and probably quite common accusation is that the missionaries "stole the land from the natives." This is completely refutable by indisputable facts available to anyone who studies missionary history.

Those good men and women did have their human weaknesses and unfortunate faults, as we view them today — their strict Puritanism, threats of the wrath of God and horrors of hell, opposition to non-productive good times and to all sorts of work or joyful activity on the sacred Sabbath. They acted according to the standards with which they had been imbued and in which they strongly believed. Today we have greater knowledge and experience and different views. When we examine the better side of their nature we find that their worthy lives far outweighed these faults. For never came more devoted, determined, self-sacrificing, kind-hearted men and women than these, many of whom ungrudgingly sacrificed the rest of their lives to extremely hard work for the people they learned to love.

Thirty-two of them each devoted from thirty to sixty years to this labor of love, contributing in all about one thousand nine hundred years of consecrated fulfillment.When devastating epidemics of measles, whooping cough, and smallpox struck the physically unprepared Hawaiian natives, it was the missionaries who saved thousands by vaccinating them and providing the much-needed proper care.

They produced prodigious results in education, moral values, social welfare, and kindly human treatment. In 1831 the mission established the first teacher-training school west of the Rocky Mountains, at Lahaina Luna, with a printing plant in 1834 to produce textbooks and the first Hawaiian newspaper. They painstakingly translated the Bible and printed it, as well as more than seventy different textbooks. They set up special schools for boys and girls to prepare them for productive lives, one to prepare chiefs' children for future rule, and Punahou School for their own children. Within just twenty years the mission had nineteen stations providing religion and education for most of the islands' people, thus making Hawai'i a Christian nation with "a higher per cent literacy than any contemporary country, including the homeland of their tutors."

Robert Louis Stevenson, at first strongly critical of the missionaries for their "deficiency of candor, humour, and common sense," came to conclude that they were "the best and most useful whites in the Pacific." The missionaries do represent the beginnings of American life with high principles in Hawai'i.

(For a more detailed study, read *Hawaii: Truth Stranger Than Fiction* by this author and *Grapes of Canaan: Hawaii 1820* by Albertine Loomis.)

❃ King Kamehameha III ❃

Photo: Hawai'i Sate Archive

Kauikeaouli was Hawai'i's longest-reigning monarch, from 1825 to 1854. Because Kauikeaouli was only nine years old when his older brother Liholiho died, Queen Ka'ahumanu served as regent until her death in 1832, when Kīna'u succeeded her. The young king so resented his half-sister as ruler that he revolted into a two–year period of dissipation, but they became reconciled by 1835.

The reign of Kamehameha III produced the bill of rights, religious tolerance, payment of the national debt, and laws for land ownership. Threats of takeover by France, England, and America were stalled. The economy turned from sandalwood and whaling toward sugar.

❋ King Kamehameha IV ❋

Photo: Hawai'i Sate Archive

Alexander Liholiho was a son of Kīna'u, a nephew of Kamehameha III (who named him as his successor), and a grandson of Kamehameha I. Angered by a racial insult on a visit to America, fearful of encroachments by American authority, and impressed by Great Britain when he visited there, as king (r. 1855 1863) he gradually enhanced British influence in Hawai'i. This attitude was supported by his Queen Emma, adopted daughter of an English physician, Dr. T. C. B. Rooke.

Chief accomplishments of the reign of Kamehameha IV were the establishment of Queen's Hospital (a result of the

royal concern over the high Hawaiian death rate from disease) and of the Anglican Church in Hawai'i. Suffering from asthma and remorse over shooting and wounding his secretary and later losing his cherished son, the king died in 1863 at age twenty-nine, after naming his elder brother, Lot, his successor.

❃ King Kamehameha V ❃

Photo: Hawai'i Sate Archive

Lot Kamehameha (r. 1863–1872) aimed to restore some of the royal power of his grandfather, Kamehameha I. At the same time, he ruled with conscientious regard for his people, refused to repeal the liquor law, and mingled so freely with the people that Mark Twain wrote that "he was popular, greatly respected and even beloved."

Unable to get agreement on a new constitution, he wrote and put into force the Constitution of 1864, which endured twenty-three years, longer than any other Hawaiian constitution — but also stirred up the opposition that was finally to overthrow the monarchy.

Lot Kamehameha never married and had no direct successor. He named his sister, Victoria Kamāmalu, to be queen, but she died in 1866. An hour before his death, he offered the throne to Bernice Pauahi Bishop, but she declined.

❋ King William Charles Lunalilo ❋

Photo: Hawai'i Sate Archive

William Charles Lunalilo (r. 1873–1874) was a descendent of a half-brother of Kamehameha the Great. He became the first elected king, since Lot had not named a successor. Lunalilo won a heavy popular vote over his one rival, David Kalākaua, and was promptly approved by the Legislature.

With three Americans in his cabinet, including Charles Bishop, husband of Princess Bernice Pauahi, as head of foreign affairs, the government favored a reciprocity treaty with the United States to help the struggling sugar interests. But when that issue became linked with ceding Pearl Harbor,

native people rose in uproar and Lunalilo finally withdrew his acceptance of the treaty.

Hopelessly ill after long periods of poor health, aggravated by his love of whiskey, Lunalilo died on his thirty-ninth birthday after reigning only twenty-five days longer than one year.

❃ King David Kalākaua ❃

David Kalākaua (r. 1874–1891) easily won election by the Legislative Assembly, defeating his single opponent, Queen Emma. A man of great talents, he revived the neglected Hawaiian culture and became the first monarch in the world to visit the United States, where his presence helped ratification of a reciprocity treaty to satisfy the eager sugar planters.

Photo: Hawai'i Sate Archive

Kalākaua was also the first monarch to travel around the world, a trip of eight months in 1881. He began construction of 'Iolani Palace in 1879 and finished it in 1882, crowning himself in a grand ceremony on February 12, 1883, the ninth anniversary of his accession to the throne.

Amid political confrontations, Kalākaua sailed for San Francisco November 25, 1890. He died there on January 20, 1891.

❃ Hawai'i Comes under American Rule ❃

American influence in Hawai'i came early, as traders in the Pacific became active in the 1820s. Even in 1820, when American missionaries arrived from New England, King Kamehameha II observed, "White men all prefer O'ahu. I think the Americans would like to have that island." Some later American missionaries left their religious calling to aid the fumbling monarchy find its place in the world of international rivalries.

In 1842, President John Tyler extended the Monroe Doctrine to include Hawai'i. With Oregon and California in American control and the discovery of gold in the late 1840s, American domination of Hawai'i became more attractive.

Annexation was proposed in the U.S. Congress in 1852 to give Hawai'i protection in time of war and to ensure this important trade route to the East. Then, in 1854, King

Kamehameha III negotiated a treaty for Hawai'i to become a state, but it was not ratified.

It was the burgeoning sugar interests that drove the Hawaiian monarchy toward an American connection. In 1872, Henry Whitney, a missionary son, proposed a reciprocity treaty with the United States by leasing Pearl Harbor. The United States was not satisfied with just a lease, and King Lunalilo was reluctant to give the harbor away.

When David Kalākaua won election in 1874, followers of his opponent, Queen Emma, became so infuriated that they staged a fierce riot. The new government, without any armed forces to protect itself, got help from two American warships and one British ship to restore order.

In 1876, a reciprocity treaty with the United States was at last signed. Still, business and professional leaders, vehemently against government corruption and profligacy, organized politically and militarily and forced a new constitution on King Kalākaua in 1887 that limited his powers and the voting rights of most Hawaiians.

In 1890, loss of the reciprocity advantage for sugar stirred up strong annexation support among Americans in Hawai'i. When the king died in 1891, his sister became Queen Lili'uokalani. She was even more determined to rule for the

Photo: Hawai'i Sate Archive

Hawaiian people, while her opponents formed the Annexationist League to keep royal power limited and see that Hawai'i became part of the United States. When the queen sought to proclaim a new constitution to restore her supremacy, the well-organized and armed forces of the annexationists took control of government buildings and declared a provisional government. U.S. forces from a warship made the takeover all the more safe and sure.

Because of this military support, President Grover Cleveland considered reinstating the queen, but the opposing forces in Hawai'i acted to set up the Republic of Hawai'i with a new constitution on July 4, 1894. The United States debated the issue of annexation until Congress, impelled by the Spanish-American War and the country's new position in the Pacific, acted on July 7, 1898, to annex the Republic, which became the U.S. Territory of Hawai'i.

Hawai'i was awarded statehood by a bill passed by Congress in March 1959 and became the fiftieth state on Admission Day, August 21 of that year.

❃ Bernice Pauahi, Charles Bishop, and the Bishop Estate ❃

Photo: Hawai'i Sate Archive

A smart young businessman, Charles Reed Bishop, came to Honolulu from Glen Falls, New York, October 12, 1846, at age twenty-four, married a lovely princess, and took a leading role in the development of Hawai'i. His marriage was on June 4, 1850, to Bernice Pauahi, a great-granddaughter of Kamehameha I and final heir to the royal lands. She was eighteen, Bishop, twenty-eight. Bernice did not inherit the royal lands until 1883, the year before she died. These lands came to her as the last living direct descendant of Kamehameha, after the death of her cousin, Princess Ruth Keʻelikōlani.

When Bernice died in 1884, these lands she had inherited, along with those she had owned and some donated by her husband, were put into the Bishop Trust to provide funds for the establishment and operation of the Kamehameha Schools for the education of native Hawaiians. The total land was 431,378 acres, about one-ninth of all lands of the kingdom. Lease of these estate lands now provides funds to support these schools. Bishop established the first bank in Hawai'i in 1858, Bishop & Co., then incorporated as Bank of Bishop & Co., Ltd., today, the First Hawaiian Bank. The Bishop Museum, opened in 1891, today stands as a monument to the Bishop and Kamehameha families. It has expanded to include all the Pacific region.

Photo: Douglas Peebles

Bishop Museum

❃ Hawai'i — Place of Many Cultures ❃

Foreign settlers began coming to Hawai'i soon after Captain Cook found the islands in 1778. By 1820, Americans, British, Scottish, French, Italians, Spanish, Portuguese, and Chinese lived in Hawai'i.

Native Hawaiians were dying out by the nineteenth century, and the growing sugar plantations needed laborers. First came 300 Chinese aboard the *Thetis* in 1852 and 1853. Thousands more followed. Japanese immigrants came in 1885 and kept coming until 1924 — nearly 200,000 of them. Europeans came, too: Portuguese started coming in 1883 — also 1,300 Germans, who assimilated well. But Norwegians soon left. By 1886, the Hawaiians were outnumbered.

Early in the twentieth century came 5,000 Puerto Ricans and 7,400 Koreans. Later came Filipinos and Okinawans, making Hawai'i the "melting pot" of the Pacific.